THE SPARROW'S PLIGHT:

WOES OF A 21ST CENTURY BLACK POET

THE SPARROW'S PLIGHT: WOES OF A 21ST CENTURY BLACK POET

Poems
by Terry *a* O'Neal

 2014

The Motion Publications edition is the first publication of *The Sparrow's Plight: Woes of a 21st Century Black Poet.*

Motion Publications edition: 2014

Library of Congress Cataloging in Publication Data

O'Neal, Terry a.
 The Sparrow's Plight: Woes of a 21st Century Black Poet.
 I. Title.
ISBN: 0-9768492-4-0

Library of Congress Catalog Card Number:
 2014907109
Copyright © 2014 by Terry a. O'Neal
All Rights Reserved
Photo cover image by The Stockton Record
Printed in the United States of America
First Edition

Dedicated to the Memory
of Carolyn M. Rodgers

CONTENTS

Introduction by Rudolph Lewis	vii
Author's Note	xiv
a poem	15
life, liberty and a pursuit…so to speak	16
montage	18
okodee mmowere	20
through the darkness of my pain	21
sands of time 'Little Black Child' sequel	22
humanity	24
and I shall proclaim	25
slave rituals unbroken	28
voice in poetry	30
the nearest exit	31
dead at 69. born again / *for Carolyn M. Rodgers*	*32*
1/15/11	34
1/20/11	35
1/21/11	36
abstract	37
the road	38
awakenings	39
disaster zone	40
says a fatherless child to her father / *for Ms. Johnson*	*41*
the closet	43
plight of Africa's child	44
thief of eternity	46
if—a crooked word	47
a matter of kindness	49
nefelibata	51

to struggle	53
home / a tribute to Aunt Lottie	55
INTERLUDE ONE	57
INTERLUDE TWO	58
INTERLUDE THREE	59
he that is in me: mourning our son (for *Sybrina Fulton and Tracy Martin*)	60
deja blues	61
for those less vain	62
fruit of the ages	63
Hallelujah and Amen Don't Make No Christian	65
patches	*68*
entrance	69
a short poem	70
Cecily, 1933	71
journey song / *for Carolyn M. Rodgers*	73
for some women	75
the sparrow's plight	78
Quotations	lxxxi
About the Author	xciii

INTRODUCTION

The Poet in Pursuit of Freedom: a Review of

The Sparrow's Plight: Woes of a 21st Century Black Poet

By Rudolph Lewis

In Terry *a* O'Neal's "The Sparrow's Plight: Woes of a 21st Century Black Poet" one discovers a master poet well-aware of poetic traditions of the Harlem Renaissance and the Black Arts Movement. As she makes notes, for example, in her poem "a matter of kindness," "i'm a poet—yes / molded by all time / 20th century greats / Hughes, Brooks, Rodgers, an' such / not to mention / i'm a mother, a wife, a teacher / among other things." It's more, however, than her historic awareness that will enthrall the reader, but it's also the unique angle—the anguish of the poet alone, the freedom sought in the midst of suffering, betrayal, and frustration—that intrigues and will cause one to read this volume, again and again. Her deft approach in rendering beauty and tragedy in the relationships of lovers, of parents and children, and all that what we owe to each other but fail to appreciate captures our imagination.

One aspect of a mature poet is the achievement of voice. It can be quarrelsome and cantankerous like a mockingbird, or dissonant and dark like a crow. Ms. O'Neal chose, however, among the feathery crew the sparrow. Maybe the tiny melodious and seemingly insignificant sparrow is indeed an appropriate metaphor for her poetic ecstatic voice. Or maybe the poet has in mind as well the well-known song "His Eye Is on the Sparrow," which views this bird as important enough to gain the attention of the divinity because it is essentially "free" and "happy." The sparrow learns songs from other birds and puts its own stamp on these songs of joy. In her "voice in poetry," O'Neal sets herself apart from the performance poets and the "hip hop per/former" who go for "dramatics," appealing primarily to the emotions. O'Neal, not inappropriately, views herself in contrast as "a classical note / accompanied by rhythmic percussion / in harmony with *poetic jazz* / arousing the consciousness." But, as we can glean from the title of this volume of poems, the poet's appreciation of joy and beauty in life is also grounded in the harsh and troubled realities wherever black life appears, either in the Americas or Africa. O'Neal confronts her audience with just this point in "a poem": people do not want in poems "sadness and grief," a "wo/mans / tales of woe." They prefer rather "what's lovely, what gleams . . . ophelia roses that bloom / a soft pink hue in spring / . . . printed ivory sheets / of hushed rhyme / line upon line." This most serious and committed poet reminds us in her "thief of eternity" that "keeper of our fate / time— / it can be merciless." In a great sense, her poems, though governed by time past, is about now in its harshest realities. In "slave rituals unbroken," the poet conjures up a past that is still with us, a past of betrayal and setbacks—"the relentless cycle of (d) words: /discord/disunity/demise." The ancestors are relentless in reminding us where we come from and where we are: "the echo of a voice from way back speaks / wisdom peeks through time / striking chords of past suffering, great struggle and / triumph . . ."

O'Neal, in a maternal guise, has fears for young black men "full of rebellion / and ripening before . . . time." Maybe as mother she sees danger for her own son, as in the poem "awakenings": "thinking he's grown / without a *whiff* / of the troubles / that accompany / a black man." Then there is the distance between parent and child, he in Galveston, an island once used as a slave port or market, where Jim Bowie bought and Jean LaFitte sold enslaved Africans. The poet writes, "my soul lay south, where / fragments of a young boy subsist / motionless, longing / to escape / life's sad realities." The themes of loss—of love, of opportunity—and betrayal run throughout this volume of poems. O'Neal writes, "shaken / is my spirit set adrift / through the gulf / where ferryboats float off / to Galveston." The "sands of time" is a most beautiful poem so much so I'm pressed to share its ending:

a decade now past, yet
unbroken remains my affection
the memories
left unfinished escort me
over waterways, through bayous and
lowlands—again
we meet face-to-face
an unlike place
no longer the "little black child" but
a young man
passed through the sands
of time

There's also the rupture between daughter and father, for whatever the reason the sociologist may delineate or whatever the explanation the psychologist might provide of its effects. Clearly, there is fury that bursts forth if only in words as O'Neal writes in "Says a fatherless child to her father": "no voice / telling me I have a choice / not to settle / for a no-good dead-beat cheat / too lazy to lift his feet / get a job—be a man / not raise his hand / to a woman." The abandoned child hurt lugs "a case / of inherited traits / stubbornness and pride / waiting to see / who will set aside one / for the greater good of two." Abandoned, the "fatherless" child is left "in solitude" with "time and its merciless ways," which *whittles* away at the self, replacing it with a false self of "half mooned smiles" attracting "passersby" while "her eyes told / half truths."

In her poem "and i shall proclaim," a homage to poet Carolyn M. Rodgers of whom I will have more to say), O'Neal draws a portrait of the social world of the black community, of the relationships among black men and women. There are too many black women unable to fulfill their womanhood because of absent black man. Why? The reality is that "half lie shackled and bound / while the other quarter / head for the border /

leaning on roadblocks / of tired stereotypes . . . twenty-five percent / free-for-all to contend." The poet proclaims in refrain "there is a shortage of brothas in the world." What does a "sista" do to escape the illusions? There's an irreconcilable uncertainty: "my sista has stumbled upon / an ethical dilemma and a choice / to live out her fantasy / of being caressed and loved." In a manner the disruptive situation is emblematic of an undeclared race war, she suggests in these lines: "it's a merciless world and / that border line was crossed / back in Brownsville / long ago."

The Brownsville, Texas Incident of 1906, only a decade or so within the era of Jim Crow, concluded with the injustice of 167 black soldiers dishonorably discharged by President Theodore Roosevelt for a crime in which none of them committed. It was just one among many and continuous example of black collective punishment. These soldiers were never sufficiently repaired though the truth of the frame up has been repeatedly revealed. The source of the tragic relationships of black men and women, O'Neal suggests by her Brownsville allusion, is not fully an internal cause brought on entirely by something lacking in the character of black men. Dishonor of black men and black life by unjust incarceration, police brutality, racial discrimination, and the steady diet of inferiority propaganda must be considered and deconstructed. Of course, there is always the needed struggle we all must engage for there is always the existential choice not to give in to stereotypes and the ubiquitous impact of racial oppression.

Neither Gil Scott-Heron nor Richard Wright could have written as poetically with such depth and beauty as Terry *a* O'Neal does with regard to two recent issues, namely, the tragedies of Fukishima and African child soldiers. I can imagine some poet might have been quite graphic when it comes to the inhuman wreckage caused by the tsunami and earthquake in northern Japan and the meltdown of six nuclear reactors. But in the nine-line poem "disaster zone," O'Neal captures the horror in words of wondrous awe:

i won't watch the news
because it's gloomy
like the sky
after the quake that shook Japan
leaving her spirit broken and bruised
ten thousand misplaced amid devastation
and bodies washed ashore
like seashells at low tide
after a storm

The same kind of photographic coupling of horror and beauty is also achieved in O'Neal's anti-war poem "plight of Africa's child." There are the lines "on the outskirts of Luanda / sit abandoned tanks / where small children play / clueless to if / they'll see another day." And then, the images of death and dying are rendered exquisitely, "digging their own shallow grave / fearless fighter / young soldier at the age of seven / trails of smoke / be your stairway to heaven." Here in both passages is imagism and passion rendered unparalleled in a call for peace and creative engagement.

I conclude this critique and admiration of Terry a O'Neal by a return to her portraits of the poet, which can be found in numerous poems in this volume. Among these is "dead at 69. born again," dedicated to Carolyn M. Rodgers (1940-2010), the Chicago-based poet and founder of Third World Press, as well as the Black Arts Movement. Rodgers, especially in her *How I got ovah*, says O'Neal, wrote "about how living while black / and a woman / wasn't easy and / how loving a world / with her in it / was hard / and her fondness of the black man / was even harder and / how she gave her life / for mere words / to seek undefined meaning / of soul existence / in an attempt / to inspire those willing to listen." In short, O'Neal contends the poet must be the "revolutionist" who sacrifices for the good of the many, of the larger ideals of community.

In "life, liberty and a pursuit…so to speak," O'Neal suggests that there's a larger community that confines the poem within narrow borders of "sensory" and "political correct/ness" and "judgment." The poet must be bold and courageous despite these societal chains. The poet must be "free to live / to dream, to love / to write." But poetry is also a means to pursue freedom in space and spiritually, to "tread barefoot along the bridge / above the Rhine, shaking hands / with kindred spirits." Intimacy can also inhibit and thwart the poetic process, as she notes in the short poem "1/15/11": "and it seemed to ease him / her love, her restraint, her presence / her life was no longer her own." She laments, in "if—a crooked word," about the uncertainty, the loss of love: "if I / travel across the world / passing out my love / on ivory paper / to men, women, children / *will he wait for me* . . . knowing / that tomorrow / may never come?"

This despair over aloneness—the fate of the poet or any artist—appears also in the poem "montage," in which she imaginatively tries to recapture the wild vigor and beauty of youth. She'd like "to ignite this glimmer of light / towards a burning flame / once again." And in "the closet," where the writer is at work with "only my typewriter, book light / and me / between four walls / and a door—shelter / from the storm." This withdrawal for the creative process destroys or undermines intimacy. O'Neal contrasts wonderfully the inner emotions of loneliness and fury with an imagined outer world of "simple pleasures of life, I dream of / bare feet chasing butterflies / whirlwind of autumn leaves / dance in the breeze / settling in summer's song." In a poem written "1/21/11," she "dreamt of sitting on the dock / barefoot / with my pen and pad by candlelight / writing my final words—my last / i love you's to the world."

I exit my introductory enthusiasm for Terry *a* O'Neal with her poem "the nearest exit." It is a poem about death and anonymity, in short, the poet's fear of failure. There is the haunting refrain, "who will dare to notice? / who will even care?" But in this moment, this whirl of fears, "a twisted web / against the winter dusk," the poet recovers "still / the circle of life / pushes on." Ms. O'Neal, as she continues her committed work, will indeed be assured again and again by many— beyond family and friends —that what she leaves behind with this volume and others that her sacrifices will not have been in vain. The larger community of poetry lovers will indeed discover that she has indeed done well and will reward her for her toils and for her pursuit of spiritual freedom in this world.

Finksburg, MD
July 2011

AUTHOR'S NOTE

*"Not dark enough, not light enough,
just somewhere dangling in between."*

Over the past two decades, I've been largely inspired by the profound works of late great poets of the nineteenth and twentieth century. Langston Hughes has been my literary inspiration since I was introduced to him in the late 1900s. I admired his ability to relate to the everyday person using thought-provoking expression and symbolism in his writing.

Since the release of my first book of poetry in 1999, I have strived to remain poised and politically correct in my approach to personal expression in an ultra-sensitive and judgmental society that finds comfort in pretending that the face of racism lives in the past and no longer mingles among us in this current day and age. I intend for my writing to speak truthfully and cross racial boundaries shedding light on the complexities of life being a black woman, a wife, a mother, a poet, a writer, a lover and a dreamer in the 21st century.

At the dawn of this new day, God granted me mental clarity, a vision and the empowerment to express myself more openly through my writing. *The Sparrow's Plight: Woes of a 21st Century Black Poet* is a depiction of my rebirth. The collection was cultivated by an enlightenment that struck me, giving me a front row seat by which to observe the world and my place in it from a bold new perspective. Though many of the poems in this collection were written over the course of the past two years, some pieces like *"To Struggle"* and *"Says a Fatherless Child to Her Father,"* were penned many years ago.

Prior to the birth of my new creation, I spent countless hours digesting the words of a female poet whom I highly admire. Carolyn M. Rodgers was a powerful heroic voice of the Harlem Renaissance and the Black Arts Movement. Rodgers spoke of black womanhood and racial identity with honesty and precision in every word. I admire her for her straightforward style, and most importantly for being that influential voice that many women of all ethnicities and cultures could relate to. While several poems in this book were inspired by Rodgers and reflect my unending run-ins with sista life, this collection encompasses depictions of personal encounters over the past three decades of my soul's existence.

TERRY A O'NEAL
February 2014

The Sparrow's Plight: Woes of a 21st Century Black Poet

poem

no one wants to hear
about sadness and grief
that floats carelessly *along*
an airborne virus
moving from this one
to that one
to me
folks are only interested in
what's lovely, what gleams
and ophelia roses that bloom
a soft pink hue in spring

no one cares about
another wo/mans
tales of woe
printed ivory sheets
of hushed rhyme
line upon line
that mirror past sorrows
in a present time

life, liberty and a pursuit…so to speak

let me be free to live
to dream, to love
to write this poem
without censorship nor
political correct/ness
fearless of judgment
by you or anyone else
who may not approve

let my voice be bold
to lift chins of the young
glisten eyes of the wise
and ring old wooden bells
far off within the bronzed shadows
of Egypt

let me be rhyme
care/less/ly prancing
from sheet to sheet
consciousness to consciousness
mixing among the dearly loved
black poets of the 1920's - Harlem, Chicago
and a small place somewhere
in Missouri

let my spirit soar un/bound
wander across ancient lands
tread barefoot along the bridge
above the Rhine, shaking hands
with kindred spirits
whom I've met along the way
un/hinder/ed
on my pursuit
verse by verse

growing young
as the day
grows
long

3/20/11

montage

there once was
a mutual lustfulness
between us

at an age when
I was not so wise
full of rebellion
and ripening before my time

a phase when
tiptoeing after dark
against my mother's will
spawn enchantment and
anticipation

an opening chapter when
you were the sparkle
in my eye--
living
was tender
so long ago

flash
after flash
a montage of scenes
fast-forward with the wind
recounting an alluring story
of our life

the present
be the reflection of
a past-time
drawn-out weary days spun
young to old
hot to cold
and the sweet taste of honey melon
to bitter fruit

okodee mmowere

i was lost in his masculinity
his brotha/ly ways
that double-edged sword
of blackness and pride
that makes one love and hate
concurrently.

there was an innate strength, yet
a radiant gentleness about him
the way he loved me
like no other man
could love a woman.

in spite of what the whole world thought of him
or what it believed he should be—
less than what he was in it
and far less than the world bestowed upon him,
i still loved him
and nothing else mattered.

                    through the darkness of my pain

I am no gypsy lady
nor a master magician
turning tricks, but
nothing more than a woman
occupied with loneliness and fury
that runs deep
on a mystical quest to
to find the x
which marks the spot

where
shall I begin
on my journey
to ignite this glimmer of light
towards a burning flame
once again?

sands of time
'Little Black Child' sequel

my soul lay south where
fragments of a young boy subsist
motionless, longing
to escape
life's sad realities

mighty blows of thunder, furious
lightening bolts
strike down upon the south
piercing the north

shaken
is my spirit set adrift
through the gulf
where ferryboats float off
to Galveston—where
water meets land and
secrets lay dormant
deep beneath the sand
amid the rich soil
influenced by our ancestors

a decade now past, yet
unbroken remains my affection
the memories
left unfinished escort me
over waterways, through bayous and
lowlands—again
we meet face-to-face

an unlike place
no longer the "little black child" but
a young man
passed through the sands
of time

8/2009

humanity

in a world that is inhumane
starving children sit homeless
crying
shattered dreams lay about the soil
rapidly dying
where the human race
no longer has a face
souls subsist
wandering
wondering
where do we go
from here?

and I shall proclaim

there is a shortage of brothas in the world:

as the overflow of liberated
hard-working
lonely sistas
do what they've got to do
to get the job done
droning that same lowly tune
with long drawn out phrases
that holler
"I can do bad all by myself...!"
knowing that
we'd much rather
put up with his *side-slipping* plays
and be miserable with him
than without—only
we're sistas and
much too proud
to beg

there is a shortage of brothas in the world:

departing by the
ones, tens, thousands
half lie shackled and bound
while the other quarter
head for the border
leaning on roadblocks
of tired stereotypes
and brittle backbones
fragments left behind
amount to a narrowing
twenty-five percent
free-for-all to contend

exchanging blows
calling my sista out her name
it's a downright lowdown dirty shame
forfeiting dignity
to an illusion of love—
an undefined moment of rapture
thirsting after
a person, place or thing
to call her own

there is a shortage of brothas in the world:

not-for-sale signs
concealed behind a daring reflection and
an alluring smile
off-limit zones
go unnoticed because
it's a merciless world and
that border line was crossed
back in Brownsville
long ago

my sista has stumbled upon
an ethical dilemma and a choice
to live out her fantasy
of being caressed and loved
(oh so well…)
with a first-class brotha
one of another
Mrs./sista/Ms.
or sit, wait and croon
that same-old played out tune

it's a downright lowdown dirty shame

to this utter sadness
this distress—this bold truth, i shall proclaim:
there is a shortage of brothas in the world

(Inspired by Carolyn M. Rodgers)

slave rituals unbroken

we come from matching bloodlines
of dark skin, unwieldy burdens and aching bones
the saddle of two-facedness
soothed by the quivering of the rolling sea
hand clapping to the beat
of its melody

a long line of double cross stitches
lead us to the same place
your story sounds like my story
only crooked slightly to the left
than the right
roots—
kinky and straight
split at the ends, light/dark skin
an age-old compilation
like a broken record that spins
in circles
heavy with inferiority and superiority
complexes

methodically sewn patterns
sketch blueprints of an orderly chaos
so as to sustain
the relentless cycle of (d) words:
discord/disunity/demise
we [you and me]
nursed by the same breast
bound by the same ties
journey down the same road

towards a bright light
a freedom of choice
the echo of a voice from way back speaks
wisdom peeks through time
striking chords of past suffering, great struggle and
triumph: *sweat blood from their backs / wept shards from their eyes / yet muster the strength to rise*
      (the legally binding definition of hard times)
all in the sake of
a revolution
that which dazzles bright before us [you and me], yet
we remain opposites that can't agree
cutting eyes of daggers
broken grins of fiery
calluses upon my soul

unshaken
from slave rituals and
subliminal ways of life
inherited by thy mother and
thy father
on dirt-stained knees
sowing a vast field of seeds
awaiting a brand new harvest
to pass along
the dim lit torch

voice in poetry

I am not performance poetry:
spoken-word-slam-champ-hip-hop per/former
standing on stage
moving folks with my dramatics
competing for state and national title
judged and awarded grand prize,
the offering of something striking to hope for.
I am what they call…
 a classical note
accompanied by rhythmic percussion
in harmony with *poetic jazz*
arousing the consciousness
spawning musings in montage
within a single
contemporary
traditional
verse—
if I shall be labeled
define me
the voice in
poetry.

the nearest exit

if my mother earth should open up
and swallow me alive—if I
melt down
sliding and dancing
my soul to vapors
drifting off to the heavens
who will dare to notice?
who will even care?
all but my dearest loved ones
of which I inhale harmonizing air
and share the strongest ties
unconditional love
in spite of
identities gone astray
who will dare to notice?
who will even care?
troubles of the world
grow older and wiser
dreams expire by the seconds/minutes/hours
weaving, spinning
a twisted web
against the winter dusk, still
the circle of life
pushes on

dead at 69. born again
for Carolyn M. Rodgers

she was growing old
her eyes dark
much lower than they were
not so long ago
her youthfulness and vigor
was left behind
alongside her songs
of sass an' blues
her paper soul
her poetic hues
and her dreams to be
even in her old skin
she was the face of beauty
from the front cover
to the end

a revolutionist
sharing secrets
with no regrets of
How She Got Ovah
about how living while black
and a woman
wasn't easy and
how loving a world
with her in it
was hard
and her fondness of the black man
was even harder and
how she gave her life
for mere words

to seek undefined meaning
of soul existence
in an attempt
to inspire those willing to listen
any who could relate
and silence tongues of hate

a woman
on a lifelong pursuit
of contentment
in a world that never once
stopped spinning
to ask her
what it was
she desired
in return

1/15/11

and it seemed to ease him
her love, her restrain, her presence
her life was no longer her own
indebted to the world
she balanced a tightrope of political correctness
seeking freedom through muted words
that didn't exist

1/20/11

sweet sounds of her laughter
came few and far between
summer days and dark stormy winter nights
spent in solitude
time and it's merciless ways
whittled away at her
while half mooned smiles attracted passerbys
and her eyes told
half truths

1/21/11

as darkness thickens
i dreamt of sitting on the dock
barefoot
with my pen and pad by candlelight
writing my final words—my last
i love you's to the world
those who cared
and those who didn't give a damn
will hear the resonance of my voice
within the stillness
as morning ash settles
upon the porch
at sunrise

abstract

must I always be the cause
of the effect:
leaving whirlwinds spinning in every footstep—

must passion weigh
a million pounds upon my soul:
drowning in a pond of
what, if's, and y's, while
tears and deep-seated fears
of abstract dark spaces
swallow me up
alive—

the road

somewhere
still shines the sun
simple pleasures of life, I dream of
bare feet chasing butterflies
whirlwind of autumn leaves
dance in the breeze
settling in summer's song
while
the midst of life looks cloudy
somewhere
still shines the sun

awakenings

he rides cool—
laying low
on his first drive
from Inglewood to
the capital city
emotionless, yet
knee-deep in thought
pondering
whoknowswhat
thinking he's grown
without a *whiff*
of the troubles
that accompany
a black man
in a contemporary world
he thinks
he knows it all, but
he's only
seventeen

disaster zone

i won't watch the news
because it's gloomy
like the sky
after the quake that shook Japan
leaving her spirit broken and bruised
ten thousand misplaced amid devastation
and bodies washed ashore
like seashells at low tide
after a storm

says a fatherless child to her father
for Ms. Johnson

plummeted
into this place
without choice
a muted voice
with eyes just like
 my father

my little love
was just not enough
for you to fight
every other battle was
the most important one

dangled between X lovers
if's and y's
color lines
a shade
unlike mine
set upon a dusty shelf
erased from your memory
where I no longer exist
dismissed—
like the many women
you laid up with
back when 8 track tapes
jammed *"…neither one of us*
wants to be the first to say goodbye…"
not a whisper in my ear

no voice
telling me I have a choice
not to settle
for a no-good dead-beat cheat
too lazy to lift his feet
get a job—be a man
not raise his hand
to a woman

i traveled through life
alongside hallow trees
and shallow graves
searching to find my way
lugging a case
of inherited traits
stubbornness and pride
waiting to see
who will set aside one
for the greater good of two
waiting for the day
to finally hear you say
my daughter
i
love you

the closet

pitch
black
space
only my typewriter, book light
and me
between four walls
and a door—shelter
from the storm
a small box
just enough legroom
for my dreams to hang
an' lay back
thoughts can let loose
loud, free,
raw an'
uncut

3/11

plight of Africa's child

families scattered and separated
a long way gone
children set adrift
some place
on the outskirts of Luanda
sit abandoned tanks
where small children play
clueless to if
they'll see another day
"come child, lay your head
upon my chest and weep
your soul into a deep, deep sleep…"

bottomless echoes
trapped in a downward spiral
war-torn, street children scream
far off over the distant hills
down a mighty stream
young lives:
homelessness
destitution
diseased
deepening poverty
murdered and enslaved
digging their own shallow grave

fearless fighter
young soldier at the age of seven
trails of smoke
be your stairway to heaven

the fight and plight of war
now a child's game
displaced
with no name
in the Great Lakes region of Africa
war-weary children sit crying
dark people lay dying
Freetown
Sierra Leone
damaged and dreary
places unknown
from the mines of Africa
rubies that glisten
the symbol—
promise of love, yet
who's going to save the children?

thief of eternity

cheat, steal and kill
effortlessly—
in spite of that
still have the power to heal, but
much too lofty
to wipe away past misdoings—the
keeper of our fate
time—
it can be merciless
that
way

if—a crooked word

if i
continue to write words
that warm hearts
enlighten souls
move spirits to dance
to my lyrical song
will he love me?

if i
give all that I have
to those in need
doing deed after deed
over a lifetime—expecting nothing
in return
without bitterness
will he honor me?

if i
dream of him everyday
and pray—
hanging onto the words
he might say
whispered in my ear
nestled beside a cozy fire
in winter
will he hear me?

if i
travel across the world
passing out my love

on ivory paper
to men, women, children
*will he wait for me…*knowing
that tomorrow
may never come?

a matter of kindness

i refuse to quarrel
forth an' back
of my sincerity, passion,
my ideals
runnin' around in circles
leads us nowhere
too fast—besides
telling you a million times over
would never bring you
the contentment
you seek

like it or not, ms. blakely
i'm a poet—yes
molded by all time
20th century greats
Hughes, Brooks, Rodgers, an' such
not to mention
i'm a mother, a wife, a teacher
among other things…
debating
simply is not
my desired pastime

your mother:
a great woman she was
in her own right—
i'm certainly not the first
to say it's so. I
admire pages of

her life story
volume upon volume
her early dreams
collect in a loft
below my bedroom
suitably
her legacy is yours to claim
rightfully so—
i hold no blame
against you for that
i ask only
that you recognize my place
hear my voice and meet me
eye to eye—as
women of words, you and I
both know
it's not what you say
but how it falls from your tongue
that moves a spirit to sway
to the rhythm of
                your beat

nefelibata

drifting through time
I can hit rewind
and find you standing right beside me
      that ear to listen
      that shoulder to lean
      my strong hand to hold—
      to console

I lay my burdens down upon you
the deepest desires of thy heart—
darkest secrets of my soul, I
spill unto you. Journey
into my psyche—
open my floodgates
free me from the melancholy winds
and rolling tides of woe—
carry me in your arms
through space
my secret window
a safe place
in the darkness of night

law of attraction
time and again
like a forever friend
magnetic energy pulls me unto you
and you to me—together we
are one.
from root to tip
I submit my all
to you

delicate dance steps
upon the clouds
swinging to

offbeat drum sounds and string tones
unchained—
moving to the syncopated rhythm
of my pulse
you are
the abstract painting upon my canvas
soft honey, creamy caramel and
lavender hues
conceal a mystery
only to be revealed
to you

slow forward,
rewind, pause…
but never stop.
line by line
time after time
dream after dream
when it's wet
you are my shelter

upon pastel ivory sheets
cosmic energy flows
my imagination goes
mystical places. I
lay my burdens down upon you
the deepest desires of thy heart—
darkest secrets of my soul
I spill unto you
again
and
again
and
again…

to struggle

time after time
people judge
by what they see
without knowing the struggle
deep-rooted within me.

I go toe to toe
with black and white
searching for the gray—
the middle—
the in-between—
street fighting colorism
open secrets remain unseen
hiding behind closed doors
of my
black world.

I contemplate my life
painting exquisite portraits
which deceive the eye
with a graceful smile
while inside I long to die.

I've battled with man
since birth
longing for him to reveal
my self-worth
his actions show me
I am not divine
his voice speaks

"I am just a man"
his hand
rapes me end-less-ly,
and I
let him—
his ears are death
to my cry
a cycle not easily broken with time
because it's too fixed in the mind
to be set free.

the higher up
the ladder I climb
the more isolated
my world becomes
without a soul—
no one
to walk a day
in my brown leather boots
sit down, have a cup of tea
and give a sista
some clarity.

home
                       (a tribute to Aunt Lottie)

as the warm wind blows
upon you beams the sun
your chariot has now arrived
your time has finally come.

    home.
    in harmony again
    with Uncle Thedo
    your mother, your father
    sisters and brothers
    a place of peace—
    where all pain, suffering, tears and crying cease forever.
    home.
    where I will see you again one day.

I freeze the image of you in my mind
and turn back time to Mason Drive
just to indulge in the simple pleasures of you
to gaze into your loving eyes
and listen to your stories of the children
once again—to take in
the warm aroma that fills each room—I
will savor every ounce—
    Mmm…the way you baked sweet cakes and pies
    taste just like heaven
    with silk ribbons that lace the sky.

home.
for us will never be quite the same

still today we rejoice in your name
though sadness weighs heavily upon thy heart
I am grateful that God chose you
to be a part of my life
here on earth
and the angel watching over us
from above.
home.

                                            Written the fifth day of July 2013

INTERLUDE ONE

In a desperate attempt to capture my fugitive spirit, I went back home—forty-five miles south of the capital city. Even though it's a small nothingness place where people find comfort in living a fruitless existence, it's a conservation burial ground for my fondest childhood memories and deepest dark secrets.

INTERLUDE TWO

The chill of morning leaves me in awe as I discover the most astounding realities about my life that have opened my eyes to what is destined to come—what my future holds. My life, from this day forth, will never be the same. In spite of this rude awakening, I continue to write because like it or not, it's what I was born to do—

INTERLUDE THREE

He is simple, yet so very complex. His movement is difficult to comprehend at times. An undying passion burns deep within his soul beneath layers of heartbreak. Like shattered pieces of glass, we get only a mere glimpse into fragments of his life. Tiny shards left behind signify the pain, struggle and emptiness which ignite his fervent desires of majestic greatness. Armored—protector of his own spirit—to shed his clothing only makes him vulnerable to the cold world. His heart bleeds through half-mooned smiles that many times go unnoticed because no one truly recognizes his struggle—no one really knows his story.

he that is in me: mourning our son
(for *Sybrina Fulton and Tracy Martin*)

i wish this throbbing pain
would go away
pounding it's ancient drum beats
down upon me

i hear bells ringing
and bugles blowing
from a distant land

the resonance of
a mother mourning her lost son
drones nearby
while a father's faith shrivels
like a rose in the desert sun dies
crying tears of blood
upon the breast of our
mother America

divided worlds roam one land
traveling down different paths
toting unlike inflexible ways
so mighty
splitting her backbone in two
leaving a part
as wide and shallow
as the red sea

Written the fifteenth day of July 2013

deja blues

if only I could turn back the hands of time
and hit rewind. I would change the lyrics
to this lowly old song and dance
to the rhythmic beating of my own heart.

the scent of tomorrow
would not linger into the brisk air of today,
and my footprints upon the ocean shore
would wash away.

for those less vain

let me not mourn the departed
nor the lifeless
of which I have no influence

alone
in a place
where the woes of the world
will carry on
long after I'm dead an' gone

who shall grieve for me
in my time of need
for what good is a heart that bleeds
in an overcrowded room
of conceit?

fruit of the ages

broken and torn
on my last leg
livin' has taken thirty years off my life
i turned into a has-been overnight
waiting on my breakthrough:
my magical time to shine

not knowing that
the dim light that glowed
back in my thirties
had already happened

i should have jumped that moving train
and never looked back
but instead
i stood there waiting on something greater--
something more miraculous

oblivious
holding onto some fantancy
not knowing that
fantasies are nothing more than fiction
and miracles happen only for the saintly
and children
neither of which
I am

i pretend
playing mind games with myself
to survive one day to the next

scouring for that bright light
or just a mere glimpse of it
holding onto a hope
like the mother back in Georgia
searching for her lost son
who went missing thirty years ago

so we continue pleading and chasing
chasing and pleading
for a moment that will never come
because like her son
my dreams vanished
to some benighted land
where tomorrow
holds no promise

Hallelujah and Amen Don't Make No Christian

i always hear folks say
"He may not come when you want..."
especially those sanctified church folk—
those Monday, Wednesday, Thursday, Friday, Sunday
church going folks.

i listened to an old women preach
trying to save my lost soul in the church parking lot
only because she earned the right
and mama always taught me to respect my elders.

tolerating the unyielding pavement
with sore feet and hollow-eyed
i heard the Sister talk this...
neverending talk
'till her voice became muted by the stirring thoughts
within the confined corners of my mind
> *because I learned to pretend to listen*
> *without really listening at all*

just standing there thinking how
if ever there was a right time
that time is now
should He wait 'till I break
before my *right on time* should arrive
there may be nothin' left of me
except ash an' bone.

between my thoughts
neverending talk intervened,
> *"Ya know, chil', He never gives you more than you can bear."*

i nodded and grinned
thinking back to yesteryears
how I consumed my fair share
of disappointment, sorrow, sucka punches and despair
from the world and
will gladly pass on another serving.

at age forty
already beaten, battered, bruised
tired of caring
and livin' this imitation life—
real troubles of the world:
all of the Sister's
neverending talk failed to mention.

so please don't try to sell me no pipe dreams
or false hopes
'cause I paid a high price for them
countless times before
only they were either used, busted or outdated
leaving me broke and penniless.

surely by now
i am wise enough to know
that quoting scriptures
hollering hallelujah and amen
don't make no Christian

or no less a sinner
in this world,
'cause mama didn't raise no fool.

patches

if it were not for the magic glue
that binds me together
i would have surely fallen a part
long ago

entrance

The door is ajar. I catch a glimpse of folks mingling--connecting in meaningful ways. Only those with special badges can gain admittance though. I'm just on the outside looking in, wishing to be something I'm not.

a short poem

Wednesday
had come and gone
in a single breath.
As I dreamt of divine love,
Picasso and a vast field of gold
a new dawn had already begun.

Cecily, 1933

like broken sticks
her legs hung
narrow and frail
bone-dry
dark skin, crimped
by merciless rays

shadows pass over
row by row
ever so slow
again

sunrise
cuttin' cane
sunset
grindin' and pressin'
pressin' and grindin'
plowing her way
toward freedom

shoo! go away!
dreaming ain't allowed here
never has been
never will

the ground trembles
mighty thunderous roars
strike the Louisiana sky

hush little children
pouting ain't allowed here
never has been
never will

journey song
for Carolyn M. Rodgers

so you ask
why
i sing?

song
gives me hope
when there's no hope
left in sight

song
passes time
it turns day
into night

song
gives me strength
when I haven't
any fight

when my legs
can no longer stand
when my hands
can no longer hold
when my soul
turns bitter and cold

song
is the prayer
that pacifies me
my song
it sets me free

for some women

i don't know.
reflecting back
only childhood comes to mind…
has there ever been a time
that I
experienced bliss?
have I ever felt true contentment?

i been sad for so long
happiness has become an intriguing stranger
i only dance with
in my dreams

destitute and desire
i call by first name
we long for the same satisfaction
that cannot be fulfilled
by material things

worn out attire
attracting nothing but moth
innocence and experience
whisper to each other,
    "a backyard burning is in order."
but no time
is ever the right time
and the right time

is obstructed by storm

i let life weigh me down
down
all the way down
to the earth beneath the feet
of both the living
and the lifeless
afraid of what comes next
knowing
it can't be worse than the present
waiting
on something miraculous
a bright white light
that never comes
left
to chose between lonesomeness and blues

weary, worn, weathered, torn
loving everyone else
neglecting myself

mother, sister, daughter, lover
of the world:
wombman

a pillar of strength
the glue that binds
everything broken together
except
me

the sparrow's plight

I desire originality and freedom of choice—though I'd never be termed a revolutionist.
I find myself at a crossroads midway along this journey, searching for the in-between world where I can close my eyes and savor. Only time keeps pushing me forward too fast. Forty settled on my doorstep just last summer, what seemed like only yesterday. And here it comes knocking again.

Words…gentle words, no longer become chocked by political unacceptableness or for kindness sake. Stream of thought is not line edited for tone, style and consistency. I have people pleased all my life—more than I care to admit.

> Calling on Greenlee, Lewis and Weems: great black writers
> of their time—of today, who say
> *"Looks like you've got it all together sista. So, the question is…*
> *what exactly can I help you with?"*
> Afraid to reply because I have no proper response other than…looks
> can be deceiving, misleading and *"I'm drowning in my words. Help me.*
> *Save me. Rescue me! My voice has gone ahead without me, desperate to be*
> *salvaged from this shallow hole I've tunneled into the earth."*

Relationships versus my passion,
like oil and water
don't mix.
In the world I live in:
a husband bound by hard-wearing love
will give his life to save my soul (and I would him) but
cannot juggle both:
fulfill my purpose and be his everything—

wearing that S upon my chest.
My soul is wearing paper thin.

His expectations deplete me. For he
cannot grasp the simplest of things…
like how desires of thy heart flows upstream…or
why I continue to float against his current…or
why I imagine and love in abstract ways—
wearing my heart upon my sleeve;
practicing humanitarianism effortlessly;
offering affection in passing because
tomorrow isn't promised and
a brotha was down on his luck,
needing to hear the soft voice of a strong, beautiful, humble, black sista say,

> "There's nothing in the world like a strong black
> man/you…and there's no other that i/we/a sista/me
> can better relate to."

                                        A brotha in utter darkness
                                        needed/needs to feel the warmth
                                        of her smile upon his chest, only
                                        my man can't understand why that
                                        soft-spoken, strong, beautiful
                                        humble, wombman need be
                                        i/we/a sista/me, and

I have no response that will bring comfort. He
often wonders why contentment can't capture me
[the love of his life]: settled in a home with a white picket fence
three children and a dog—domesticated
in a space where
gender roles receive standing ovations

in this…*liberated woman of the 21st century world;*
and y we can't love and like in unity,
living happily eva after
in a perfect world
until
the
end.

~Quotations~

"It's a thorny road for dreamers and poets who fantasize of majestic places and deep-seated desires of the heart that their hands may never hold."

"It's easy to get caught up in where the world is going and lose sight of the direction we were headed."

"I've learned to utilize poignant memories—the most heartbreaking moments in life which move me to tears at a glimpse of thought."

"When life weighs heavy upon my shoulders and patience starts wearing thin, it is divine hope and dreams which sustain me, pushing me forth against the wind."

"Oftentimes, I find myself amazed at how humanity can overcrowd a colossal universe, yet loneliness is a ubiquitous phenomenon."

"All I ever really wanted to do was arouse souls through my writing and enjoy my journey to becoming one with myself and with the world."

"Trying to pump breath into a fairy tale is as arduous and tragic as ancient Greek theatre."

"Yes, it is true that beauty is only skin deep, and internal loveliness resonates to the outside; but deep down inside every woman secretly longs to possess the allure of a royal queen."

"It is true that internal woe dulls the vibrancy of space. So why must every corner adorn forty shades of violet blue with whispers of sea green?"

"We will awaken—we together. So much is telling us our story and its beauty…and seeing you take root into being the tree of life that you are."

"Isolation filled with loud silence is a writer's paradise. I wonder how far north toward the Mediterranean must I travel to get there."

About the Author

Terry a O'Neal is best known as a literary mentor and activist in the literature community. Novelist and poet Terry a. O'Neal has sought to spread words across a dying nation of eager listeners. Her unending passion and persistent dedication in forcing humanity to see the truth has become the platform of her journey.

O'Neal began her path of writing in her early twenties. Having first-hand experienced the struggles of what it means to feel alone in a crowded world, O'Neal exemplifies tenacity. The mentorship she provides for the youth of this generation is by far a treasure in itself. O'Neal not only extends her loyalty of language through programs geared towards students, but through various outlets in the community and around the globe. From the authentic grounds of Jamaica to the Pelican state of Louisiana where her roots lie, O'Neal has left a major impact of inspiration on a constant changing world.

O'Neal is a reputable writer of fiction, poetry, children's literature and screenplays. Her novels and poetry represent real-life issues, including the struggles of a family learning the pain of adultery and forgiveness in *Sweet Lavender,* which has been adapted into the feature film *Along the Dirt Road.*

Her contributions to literature include, *Motion Sickness,* her first book of poetry that was released in 2000 through her own company, Motion Publications. Terry a. O'Neal's collection of vibrant writings also includes –*The Poet Speaks in Black (2002), Ev'ry Little Soul (2002), Good Mornin' Glory (2006),* and *My Jazz Shoes (2007).* All of these literary vibrancies are mere products of one individual pushing past her own struggles to help release the dreams of humankind. Her offerings of scripted sacrifice plunges into mainstream literature, while providing a charismatic energy to those that follow.

Terry *a.* O'Neal has sought to use education in reaching her goals of success. With a Master of Arts in Education and her current PhD studies in the field of social psychology, her determination to motivate like-minded writers will provide the strength many need to withstand the constant climb up the ladder of success.

Amongst many hats, she is the founder and educator of the National Black History Bee that is presented to adolescence in inner-city schools as a contribution to African-American history. O'Neal serves as the vice president and integral voice of the nonprofit organization *Lend Your Hand, Inc.*, an association that provides disadvantaged youth with the proper school supplies and resources to help make learning a success.

O'Neal's desire is to bring the power of humanity as close as possible to the heart of youthful minds; and as spoken from the philanthropist herself, "*to make a difference in the lives of others through my writings and humanitarian efforts.*"

Toi Nichelle
Author of *Mirror to my Soul* and *The Hush Language*
Dream Loud Ink Publishing
February 2014

www.ingramcontent.com/pod-product-compliance
Lightning Source LLC
Chambersburg PA
CBHW060204050426
42446CB00013B/2985